The Story of Power

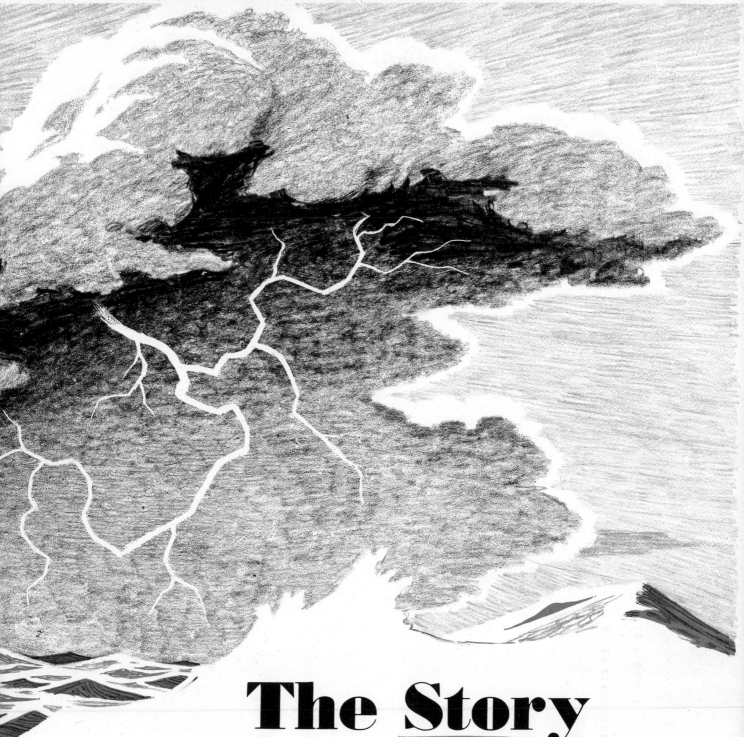

The Story
of POWER

BY EDWARD STODDARD

Illustrated by Lee Ames

DOUBLEDAY & COMPANY INC., GARDEN CITY, N.Y.

The author's thanks to Guy S. Longobardo, Instructor in Mechanical Engineering, School of Engineering, Columbia University, for checking the accuracy of the manuscript of this book.

Contents

U. S. 1174090

How We Use Power

THE WORLD we live in depends on power.

Power drives ocean liners and cargo ships across the sea. It lifts airplanes into the sky. It pulls trainloads of passengers and freight across the country. It lifts elevators and runs refrigerators and pulls plows and works lights. It makes cars and busses and trucks go. It runs radios and television sets.

Every time you push a button or turn a switch or pull a lever that makes something happen, you are putting power to work.

And power does many other things just as important but not quite as often noticed in our daily lives. Power runs the factory machines that make almost everything we wear or use. Power looms weave the cloth in our clothes. Power saws and drills shape our furniture and make our houses. Power cutters, stamps, presses, mold our cars and bicycles and pots and pans.

Without power we could never go farther than we could walk, or faster than we could run. Without power we would never own anything except what men could make with their own muscles.

Without power we would still be savages.

We get power in many different ways. We get power from running water and burning coal, from the wind and burning gasoline.

We turn running water and burning coal and exploding gasoline into power by using engines and motors of many different kinds. Complicated as they seem, they all work on just a few simple principles. What they do and what goes on inside them is a wonderful and exciting story.

7

Where Power Comes From

EVERY KIND of power except atomic energy—whether our muscles, or steam engines, or electric motors, or jet planes—came from the sun.

There are only four ways in which we get power: from the wind, from flowing water, from burning fuel, and from atoms. All of them except atoms got their power from the sun.

The wind blows because the sun heats some parts of the earth more than others. The warm air rises. Cool air from other places rushes in to fill the gap left by the rising air. This air rushing from one place to another is the wind. The power to make it blow came from the sun, which warmed the air and made it rise in the first place.

Water running downhill gives us much of our electric power. But before water can run downhill, it has to get to the top. Water gets to the top of the hill by falling as rain. Rain, of course, comes from clouds. The water vapor, or steam, to make the clouds comes from oceans and lakes.

8

The heat of the sun's rays shining on the oceans and lakes turns some of the water into vapor. Every day the sun's heat silently and invisibly draws millions of tons of water up through the air as vapor.

So when we get power from running water, that power also came from the sun.

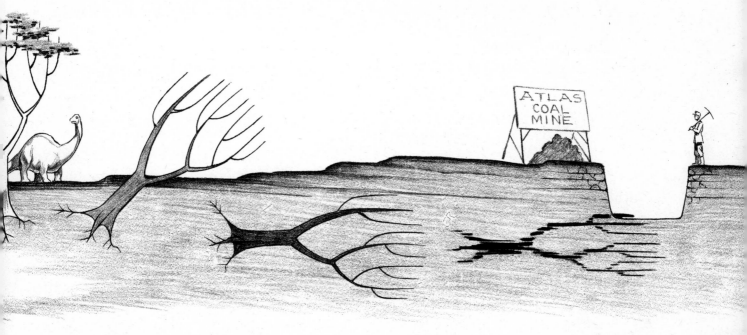

The third way in which we get power is by burning fuel.

The only substances that will burn are "organic" substances—things that were once living plants.

Rock is not organic, and will not burn. Coal, which looks like rock, will burn. But coal is not rock. It is really wood from trees that lived millions of years ago. The trees rotted and were pressed into coal by the rock formations that centuries piled on top of them.

Oil and gas are also "organic." They too are made of plants and tiny animals that lived ages ago. Gasoline, diesel oil, jet fuel, and other fuels are made from oil.

Every fuel comes from something that was once alive.

There is another kind of burning that releases power. This is the burning of sugar in the muscles of men and animals. When you lift something, the power that moves your muscle comes from sugar being burned inside the muscle.

* * *

"Organic" substances burn because they have power locked inside them, power that came from the sun.

Green plants capture this power from the sun by a chemical process called photosynthesis. "Photo" means light. "Synthesis" means make. Photosynthesis means to make by using light.

Green plants combine chemicals from water and air to make organic substances. They can do this only with the power of sunlight. Other living things, such as men and animals, get their food from green plants. In this way, all life depends on photosynthesis.

When an organic substance burns, it is torn apart. The chemicals return to water and air. The power locked into the substance is let go as heat.

So the heat of any fire came, in a roundabout way, from the sun.

Atomic energy is quite different. Atomic energy comes from the destruction of matter itself. Matter is actually turned into energy by tearing apart the atoms of which it is made. Atomic power is still in a very crude stage, but it will play an important part in our world in the years to come.

10

The First Engine

THE FIRST ENGINE used by man was his good right arm.

Whatever had to be lifted, or pulled, or carried he had to do himself.

Pretty soon he got bright enough to use muscles other than his own. He captured enemies in war, and made them do the heavy work. He noticed that the dogs he had tamed for hunting had strong muscles, and began to tie their leashes to things that needed pulling. He found and tamed other animals that seemed made to order for many of his jobs—horses, oxen, camels, donkeys, elephants.

Muscles are not engines as we think of them, of course. The story of power is really the story of mechanical power, which is only about 200 years old. But men have been pretty civilized for about 15 times that long, and except for wind and water the only power they had was that of muscles.

The pyramids of Egypt were built with the muscles of slaves. The great castles and churches of Europe were built with human muscles. The Great Wall of China was built by soldiers and slaves.

But men were cheap in those days. Prisoners and slaves were cheaper than animals. As men became more civilized, they began to worry about using other men as machines. It just wasn't right.

11

Animal muscles were the "engines" of our world until very recently. Oxen pulled covered wagons across America. Horses pulled the buggy that served your great-grandfather as a car, the coach that was his bus, the wagon that was his truck. Horses pulled the plows on our farms. Even the streetcars, though they ran on rails, were pulled by horses.

Animal muscles are still important engines in many parts of the world today. Elephants carry teak logs in Burma. Water buffaloes pull plows in India and China. Camels carry freight in Arabia. Dogs pull milk carts in Holland, while goats pull them in Greece.

But muscles are not very good engines. They get tired and have to rest. They use fuel, such as hay, whether or not they are working. Sometimes animals just don't want to work, and have to be managed. And they are not strong enough for the work our complicated world needs done. We have engines of thousands of horsepower. Nobody could manage a team of a thousand horses.

Men had to find other ways of getting power before they could make the world we have today.

Water Runs Downhill

RUNNING WATER was probably the first way man found to save his own muscles. It is still a very important one.

One day a cave man bringing wood for his fire found that logs would float along more easily than they would drag. Perhaps he discovered this when he waded out to pull in some logs that had fallen into a stream.

The big discovery came when he noticed that they kept moving downstream even when he let go. This must have happened many times before he got around to noticing it. When he finally got the idea, he learned to do as much wood gathering as he could upstream from his home. Now all he had to do was walk along beside his logs and take them out when they were as near as the stream went to his camp.

Finally, he decided that he didn't have to walk along with the logs, either. He made his wife wait where the logs were to come out, while he went upstream and dumped them in. Most of them got down to the faithful wife, who dragged them out again.

This is a crude form of power. But it is definitely power. Something is being moved from one place to another without anyone lifting a finger.

We still use water power in this very same form today. Most lumber companies use rivers to take the logs from where the trees are cut to the sawmill. Often they make artificial streams of wooden troughs, called flumes, to carry the logs where water doesn't happen to be running naturally.

Cargo, too, has been carried for centuries by drifting downstream on rafts or boats. Stone for the Egyptian pyramids was carried down the Nile River this way. When

13

the American Midwest was settled, the Mississippi was an important highway for keelboats and flatboats drifting down to New Orleans with goods to sell. The pioneers used muscles to get the boats back up the Mississippi, but on the trip down they sat back and took it easy while running water did the work.

*   *   *

The next big step was to harness running water and make it do work in one place. Men had lots of work to do besides gather logs. Once they learned to grow crops instead of just hunt for a living, one of their most backbreaking chores was irrigating, or watering the vegetables and grain.

Somewhere beside a river in China, or India, or Egypt, someone first thought of dipping water from the river and pouring it into a ditch running through his garden.

After years of wearily climbing up the river bank with clay pots of water, one smart farmer fastened his pot to the end of a pole. Now he could stand at the top of the bank and reach for the water without climbing down.

*   *   *

Inventions always come slowly. Most people just do things the way they have always been done. It is only when someone has the courage to wonder if there might not be a better way that progress is made.

So it was probably his grandson or his great-grandson who got tired of holding the whole weight of the pole and the pot. He made the pole twice as long and rested the center on a forked pole. Now he could raise it and lower it with much less work.

Another grandson noticed that when he raised the end with the pot, the other end of the pole went down into the water. After some pretty hard thinking, he fastened a pot to the other end. Now he could raise about twice as much water with the same number of motions.

It was probably a long time before anybody made the next big step: adding another cross-pole and connecting the whole thing to the stake so it would turn around and around like a wheel.

With pots at each end of each pole, and a trough that would catch the water from each pot when it came to the top and began spilling, the farmer now had a sort of wheel pump. Instead of having to raise and lower a pole, someone could just keep turning the wheel around and around.

There are still wheel pumps like this in China. Some of them are so big that several farmers climb on top and walk on the spokes, like a treadmill, to turn the wheel.

14

One day after heavy rains had swollen the river and the current was running fast, someone noticed that one of these wheels was turning all by itself. The running water, pressing against the part of the wheel that was in the water, made it turn slowly.

All he had to do was add paddles so the current could grip the wheel better, and he was in business.

The water wheel had been invented.

As long as the current ran, the wheel turned and lifted water to the garden. Nobody had to strain a muscle.

*   *   *

Nobody knows if this is how the water wheel was really invented. But it must have happened more or less like this.

When mills were invented to grind flour by turning one stone on another, slaves and animals were used to turn the stone. Then someone thought of harnessing the water wheel. The wheel did not have to be fed and it never got tired.

The mechanical looms of early New England cloth factories were run by water wheels. So were the spinning wheels in thread factories. Many sawmills were powered by running water.

*   *   *

Today water wheels are not used very much in America. But the power of running water is one of our most important natural resources. We build great dams such as the Grand Coulee and Hoover dams largely for the power they will produce.

Running water is used today to make electricity. Such a plant is called a hydroelectric station. It uses a highly efficient kind of water turbine that turns a generator, or machine that makes electricity. A turbine is a kind of water wheel enclosed in a jacket that controls the flow of water. Because the water is directed and controlled by the jacket, the turbine is far more efficient than an ordinary water wheel.

The generator turned by the turbine supplies electricity to factories, railroads, homes, and other users of current. About one fourth of the power in our country comes from running water. Your power company may buy the electricity from a hydroelectric plant miles away.

The only thing wrong with hydroelectric power is that there just isn't enough of it. There isn't enough water running down steep enough hills to give us all the power we need.

The Wind Is Free

MEN must have learned to use the power of the wind almost as soon as they began making water work for them.

Perhaps a cave man floating logs down-river to his camp had to get them across a lake where there was no current. So he sat on one of them and paddled it across. But then, one windy day, he found that he kept moving even when he stopped paddling. The wind pressing against his back shoved him along.

This was a strange and wonderful thing, much harder to understand than the running water he could actually see moving. And since the wind was not always blowing, or blowing in the right direction, it was not as easy to use as the river current.

But slowly, his grandsons and great-great-grandsons began to make the wind work for them. One of them learned to hold a leafy branch over his head when the wind was blowing right, to catch more of it and make him move faster. Another tried holding up a bearskin to catch still more wind, and was astonished at how much faster he went. When cloth was invented, the sail could be made bigger. Sailors learned how to fasten it to sticks called masts to save their arms the work of holding it up all the time.

The sail was man's first important use of power. At first seamen knew how to sail only if the wind was blowing in the direction they wanted to go. If the wind was in the wrong direction, they just waited until it changed, or else they paddled.

It was around Columbus' time that European sailors learned how to sail where they wanted to go, no matter how the wind blew. Legends say they learned this trick from the Arabs, who learned it from the Chinese. How the Chinese discovered it is anybody's guess.

The trick is to catch the wind in such a way that part of its force pushes the ship forward. This won't work if you try to sail directly into the wind, but you can sail at an angle into it. To reach a port directly to windward, you sail back and forth until you reach it. This is called "tacking."

19

In order to tack, the sail is held slantways instead of square across the wind. The wind tries to push the sail to the side instead of just back. Since the boat is pointed to one side of the wind, this pushes the boat partly sideways and partly forward. But the boat, because of its shape, won't move sideways very easily. Instead, it moves forward. The sideways pressure makes it lean over.

Sails were the power for man's great age of exploration, when the world was mapped and new continents and islands were discovered. Sails moved people and goods across the ocean to settle America. They carried the world's trade and powered the fleets of all the navies. They were important right into our own century. After all, the wind is still free.

The trouble is, the wind may be free but it isn't always there.

The famous clipper ships of the mid-1800's were fast. Some of them went faster than 20 miles an hour with a good wind. They passed up the lumbering, puffing steamships of the time as if the steamships were standing still.

But next day it might be dead calm. The lumbering, puffing steamship kept plugging away. Like the hare and the tortoise, it came in first.

So gradually the great sailing ships found fewer and fewer cargoes. Products in the hold of a ship couldn't be sold. They had to be on the market as soon as possible. Although there were still a lot of big sailing ships during the early 1900's, even into the 1920's, they carried only the cheapest cargoes.

Today sails are used almost completely for pleasure boating. They still carry cargoes in some sleepy, unhurried parts of the world such as the Bahama Islands, but in most parts of the world the only boats that still harness the wind are yachts.

*   *   *

Just as with running water, men found that the wind could be used to turn a wheel as well as push things.

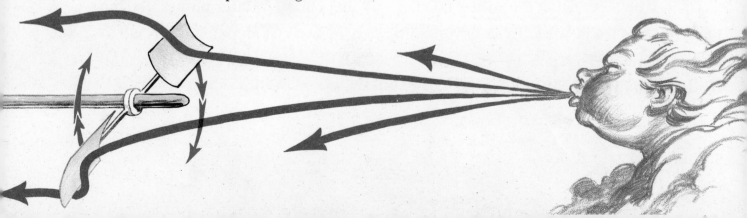

Windmills are a much later invention than water wheels. They seem to have been developed around 1100 in Germany or Holland. Today Holland is still dotted with big windmills that pump water or turn grindstones.

Dutch windmills use canvas sails stretched over wood lattice frameworks. When the wind is too strong, the sails can be rolled up. When the wind gets lighter, the sails are unrolled more.

Windmills work very much as do a ship's sails in tacking. The windmill sails are mounted at an angle to the wind. Most of the wind's force is spent trying to press the sail backward. Since the sail won't go backward, just as a ship won't move easily sideways, the only way the sail can go is around.

The biggest problem with a windmill is to keep it facing the wind. When the wind changes direction, so must the windmill.

Dutch windmills have another little windmill mounted on the back of the building. It is connected to a wheel that turns the big windmill around. Ordinarily the little windmill is at right angles to the wind and doesn't turn. If the wind changes, it turns the little windmill, which turns the big windmill until the little windmill is again at right angles to the wind.

The other important type of windmill is that used on farms. Many farms in America still have windmills to pump water from a well into the water trough for cattle or horses.

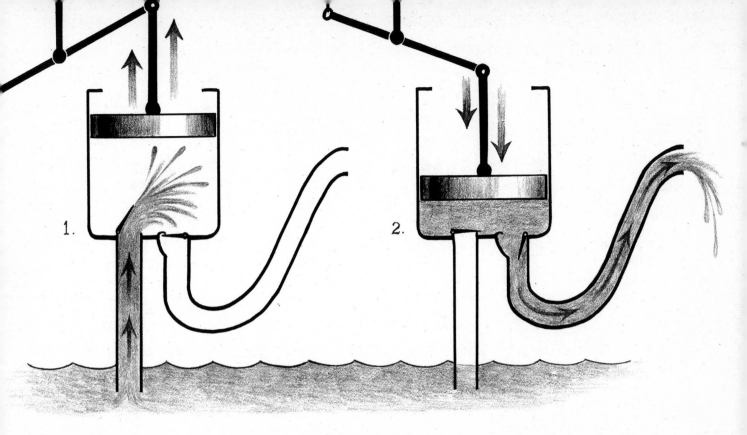

1.

2.

A Dutch windmill is big. Sometimes the wheel is 60 feet across, and it turns slowly. An American windmill is small, with a wheel only 10 feet across, and turns quickly. The wheel is usually mounted at the top of a high tower, and turns a crank which is connected by a long rod to a regular hand pump at the bottom of the tower.

The pump is made with a cylinder, or hollow tube, and a piston, or round plug that fits tightly inside the cylinder and slides up and down inside it. When the piston moves farther into the cylinder, it makes the space inside smaller. When the piston slides the other way, the space inside the cylinder gets bigger.

In the closed end of the cylinder are two valves, or doors, that can be opened and closed. One valve opens when the piston moves up. Since the space inside the cylinder is getting bigger, it sucks water up from the well and into the cylinder. When the piston moves down, the first valve slams shut and another one opens. The water in the cylinder is pushed through the second valve into the pipe leading to the water trough.

American windmills have many small wooden "sails," or blades. They cannot be rolled up when the wind gets too strong. Instead, American windmills have a tail that keeps them facing the wind. The tail can be folded back to hold the wheel at an angle when the wind gets too strong.

Windmills have never done much except pump water or grind wheat. As a power source, they are as unreliable as sails on ships. The day may come, though, when coal and oil become scarce, when windmills may be developed to provide electricity.

Steam Comes Along

RUNNING WATER is cheap and pretty dependable, but before electric power it had to be used where it was. Wind is cheap, but it isn't dependable at all. Yet these were the only forms of power other than muscles until the steam engine was invented.

The standard story is that an English boy named James Watt was watching the lid of his mother's tea kettle bounce up and down, and decided that steam could be put to work. This was supposed to have happened around 1750.

Actually, steam engines of a sort had been doing useful work in England at least 50 years before then.

The early English steam engines were crude. Like almost every other kind of power used in one place, they mainly pumped water. They were invented for pumping out the English coal mines, which kept flooding and had to be drained all the time.

*   *   *

Men had known for a long time that steam could do work, if only someone could figure out how to harness it. Steam takes up a lot more room than the water it came from. If the steam is closed in, it can push against things.

In the Newcomen engine, as it was called, the steam pushed against air. This engine began sucking the water out of English mines about 1700.

The Newcomen engine was a little like a pump worked backward. There was a cylinder, or hollow tube. A piston, or plug, slid back and forth inside the cylinder. In a pump the piston is pushed back and forth mechanically in order to suck something. In the Newcomen engine the piston was sucked back and forth in order to push something mechanically.

Steam was let into the cylinder of the Newcomen engine and pushed out all the air. The valves were closed. Then cold water was sprayed into the cylinder. The cold water made the steam condense, or turn back into water. This sucked the piston into the cylinder with enough power to work a pump.

To get the piston back, more steam was let into the cylinder. As soon as the steam rushed in, the piston was pulled back by a weight.

24

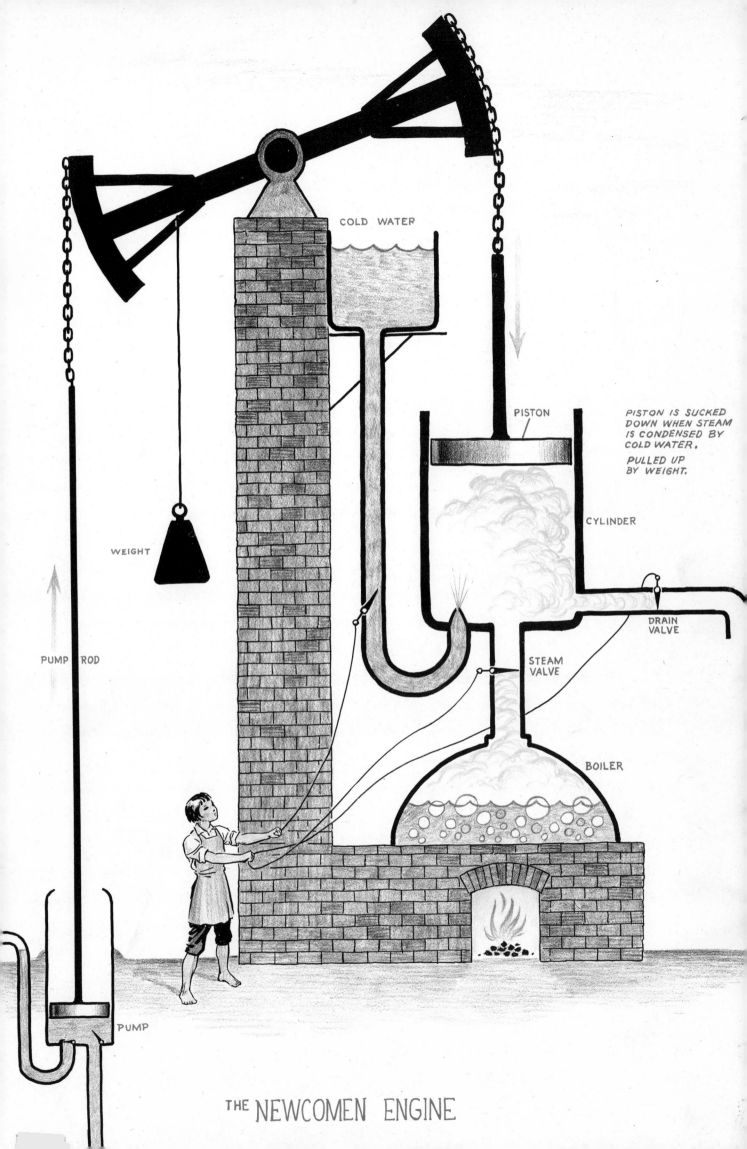

COLD WATER

PISTON

PISTON IS SUCKED
DOWN WHEN STEAM
IS CONDENSED BY
COLD WATER.

PULLED UP
BY WEIGHT.

CYLINDER

WEIGHT

DRAIN
VALVE

PUMP ROD

STEAM
VALVE

BOILER

PUMP

THE NEWCOMEN ENGINE

Someone had to be hired to open and close the valves. The engine worked only as fast as the valves were opened and closed.

The story goes that a boy named Humphrey Potter was hired around 1713 to be "valve boy" at one of the mines. Being both smart and lazy, he soon figured out that the engine might as well open and close its own valves. So he fastened some strings from the valve handles to the rods of the engine so that the valves opened and closed at the right times.

As soon as he had his connections right, the engine began huffing and puffing away many times as fast as it ever had before. This bothered Humphrey's boss and, so the story goes, he was fired.

But he had made a great invention, fixing an engine so it takes care of itself. No man could possibly handle the valves on a modern high-speed engine.

*   *   *

James Watt worked out the next big step. He made the steam engine several times as efficient as it had ever been before.

First, he realized that cooling the cylinder to condense the steam wasted power. The Newcomen engine gobbled tons of coal and didn't really do much work. Much of the power was wasted heating and cooling the cylinder. Why not, thought Watt, keep the cylinder hot all the time, and pipe the steam to a separate "condenser," or cold place where the steam would be turned back into water?

Second, Watt used steam to push the piston, instead of condensing steam to suck it. Watt was the first to use steam under pressure. He made his boiler and cylinder strong enough to keep the steam from expanding. This made the steam develop pressure and push hard on the piston.

Watt also had the idea of making the back-and-forth movement of the piston turn a shaft, or rod. If his engine could turn a shaft, it could do many other things besides pump water. It could run factory machines and perhaps—this was a daring thought—perhaps it might even drive wagons and boats! The back-and-forth movement of the piston is changed into the turning movement of a shaft by an ordinary crank. The piston is connected to the crank with a connecting rod.

Watt's engine began running around 1770. It needed more perfecting, but it was so much better than the Newcomen engine that he set up a factory to make them.

Soon steam engines began doing hundreds of jobs. They pumped out mines. They

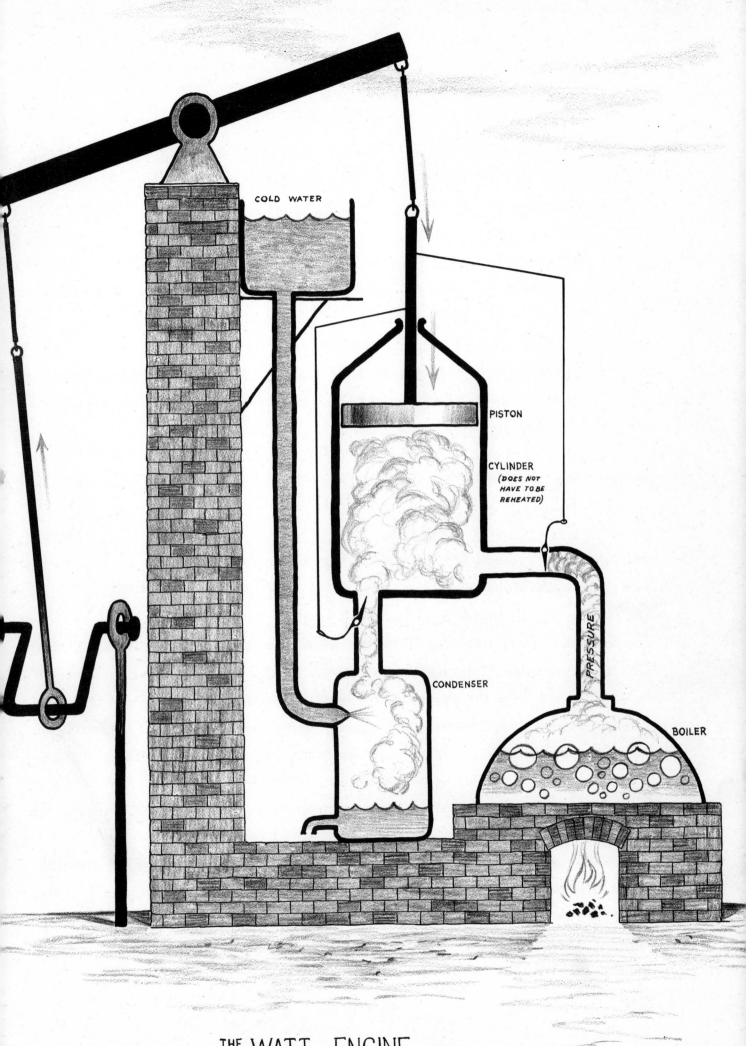

COLD WATER

PISTON

CYLINDER
(DOES NOT
HAVE TO BE
REHEATED)

CONDENSER

PRESSURE

BOILER

THE WATT ENGINE

ran sawmills and flour mills. They drove the machines in many factories. By 1800 there were a few experimental railroads and steamboats.

*　　　*　　　*

All during the 1800's steam power was being perfected and put to new uses. Railroads inched their way across America. Steamships became faster and better, and began to take the place of sail. Steam engines ran factories, lifted and hauled all sorts of heavy things, and gave their name to such handy tools as steam rollers and steam shovels—which don't run on steam any more.

Modern steam engines often pipe the used steam into a condenser. This is a tank filled with many small pipes with cold water running through them. When the steam touches these cold pipes, it is suddenly turned back into water. Since the water takes less space than the steam, the condenser has a vacuum, or pressure lower than the air. This makes it easier to push the piston back after the pressure stroke of the steam, and increases the power.

Modern boilers are far different from the simple tank with a fire under it used by Newcomen and Watt. Now the water is boiled quickly by going through many pipes in the fire, or by having the fire go through pipes in the tank of water. This heats the water much faster, so ships can "get up steam" in only a few hours instead of a whole day.

Most steam engines used today are double-acting. This means that both ends of the cylinder are closed, with the piston rod coming out one end through an airtight opening. Both ends of the cylinder can be used to push the piston back and forth with steam, instead of just one. In a way this is like having two steam engines in one.

Although the steam engine is still used, it has already become old-fashioned. Every year steam locomotives are replaced with more powerful and more efficient Diesel locomotives. Ships are turning from steam engines to steam turbines or Diesel engines. Factories get their power through electric wires instead of from their own boilers and engines. Steam-electric plants, which make most of our electricity, run on high-speed turbines instead of piston and cylinder engines.

The steam engine brought in the age of mechanical power, but like an old pioneer, it has outlived its usefulness for many needs. It is heavy and big and needs a lot of care. It can't run fast enough for many needs. Worst of all, it usually isn't very efficient. Most steam engines get only about one eighth of the power of the fuel into the crankshaft.

28

The Gas Engine

EVEN while the steam engine was still young, in the early 1800's, some engineers thought they could make a better engine.

They wanted to get rid of that big, heavy boiler. They didn't want to pipe steam under pressure to the cylinder. They thought they could burn the fuel right inside the cylinder itself. The controlled explosion of the fuel would drive the piston, just as steam pressure pushed it.

Because they would burn the fuel inside the cylinder, they called this type an "internal-combustion" engine. The steam engine is an "external-combustion" engine, since the fuel is burned outside the cylinder.

As early as 1823 very crude internal-combustion engines were made. They didn't work well enough to take the place of the steam engine, but they were a start.

From around 1870 on real progress was made. In 1876 a man named Otto invented the 4-stroke system used today in most gasoline engines. His engine didn't run on gasoline, though. There was no such thing as gasoline then. His internal-combustion engine ran on gas, the same sort of gas used today for cooking.

Otto solved the problem that had been baffling the engineers for years. They all realized that four steps had to take place in such an engine, but they couldn't work out a way to do all of them. First, fuel and air had to get into the cylinder. Second, it had to be squeezed so it would explode under pressure. Third, the explosion had to push the piston down. Fourth, the burned gases had to be cleared out, or exhausted, so a new mixture could be pumped in.

Otto's engine did all these things by itself. It did them by making the piston travel four times the length of the cylinder for each power stroke. That is why it is called a 4-stroke engine. Practically all modern gasoline engines are 4-stroke.

The first stroke is the intake stroke. The piston moves down in the cylinder, pulled by the weight of the flywheel, which keeps turning for some time even when nothing is turning it. A valve lets fuel and air come into the cylinder, sucked by the piston's movement.

The second stroke is the compression, or squeezing, stroke. The flywheel keeps turning and the crank pushes the piston up again. The intake valve is closed. The fuel-and-air mixture is compressed inside the cylinder.

30

As soon as the piston reaches the top of the cylinder, a spark plug lights the fuel. The explosion drives the piston down. This is the third stroke, the power stroke. The piston is pushing the crank instead of the crank pushing the piston. The spark plug simply lets electricity jump across the gap between two wires, making a spark.

The fourth stroke is the exhaust stroke. As the flywheel pushes the piston up again, an exhaust valve is opened. The burned gases rush out into the exhaust pipe.

When the piston reaches the top, the exhaust valve closes and the intake valve opens again, ready for the intake stroke.

Someone once described the Otto cycle as: suck, squeeze, pop, phooey.

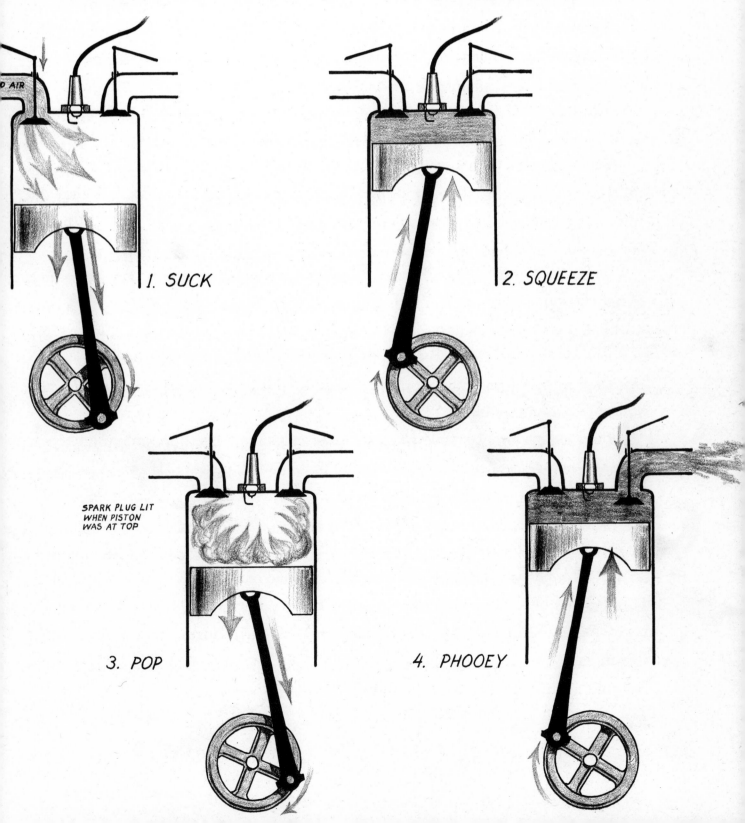

1. SUCK

2. SQUEEZE

SPARK PLUG LIT
WHEN PISTON
WAS AT TOP

3. POP

4. PHOOEY

A little before 1900 someone took another look at Otto's engine and thought of the waste product from fuel oil: gasoline.

Petroleum had been refined for years to get the thick oils such as kerosene that burned so nicely in furnaces and boilers and lamps. Nobody had much use for the light leftovers such as gasoline. It burned too fast and it evaporated too quickly for their needs.

But since it burned so fast, and evaporated so quickly, it made a perfect fuel for Otto's engine. Only one more part was needed: a carburetor.

A modern carburetor is very complicated, but its only job is to mix quickly a thin spray of gasoline with a lot of air. The many parts are to make sure that the right amount of gasoline is mixed with the right amount of air for different power needs.

Today's gasoline is far different from the early waste product. For one thing, ordinary gasoline burns far too fast. It goes off with a bang in the cylinders, causing knocking. Tetraethyl lead was added to make it explode more slowly. "High-test" gasolines with high-octane ratings have been invented recently. The octane rating is a measure of how slowly the gasoline explodes, and how much it can be squeezed without exploding by itself.

The gasoline engine made possible America's fabulous automobile industry. It brought tractors to our farms and put the horse out to pasture. It made airplanes practical. The gasoline engine did for road and air travel what the steam engine did for rails and ships.

Almost all modern gasoline engines have four, six, or eight cylinders instead of just one. This helps the engine turn smoothly, instead of with a series of thumps. More cylinders do not always mean more power, though. The power depends on the total size of the cylinders and how fast the engine is designed to run, not on the number of cylinders.

*   *   *

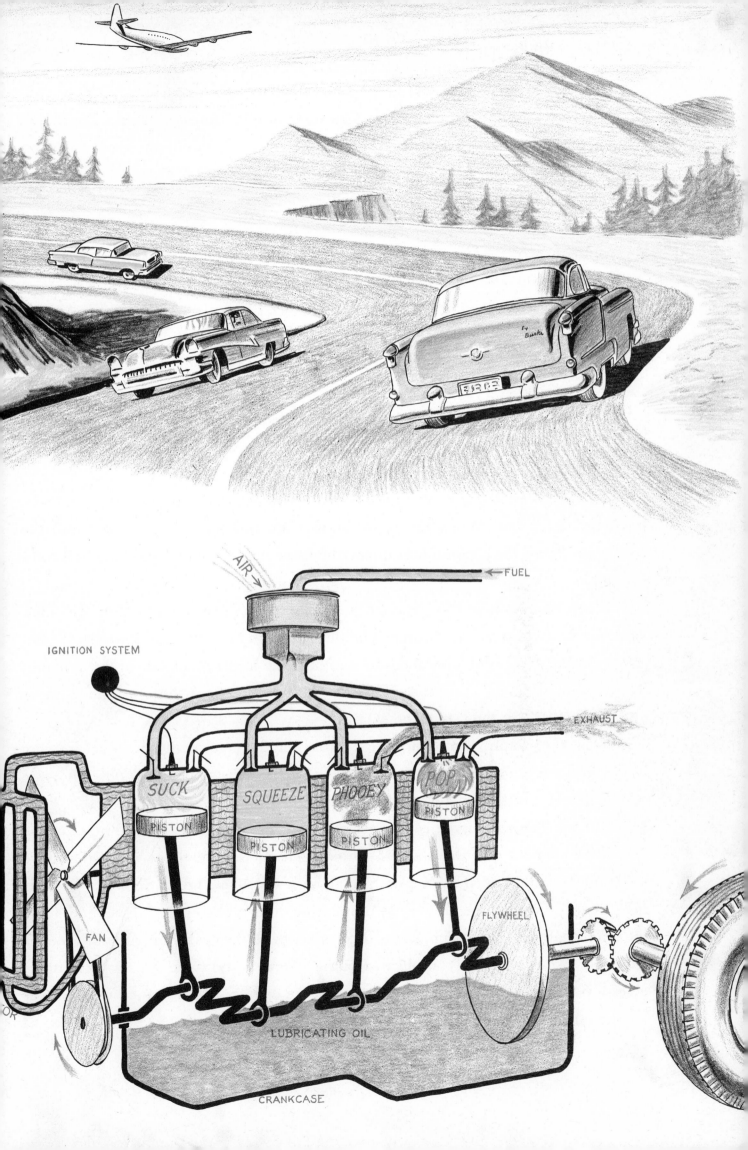

IGNITION SYSTEM

AIR

FUEL

EXHAUST

SUCK
PISTON

SQUEEZE
PISTON

PHOOEY
PISTON

POP
PISTON

FAN

FLYWHEEL

LUBRICATING OIL

CRANKCASE

There is another, simpler kind of gasoline engine that has given us outboard motors, power lawn mowers, model airplanes, and many other light, small, but powerful machines. This is called a 2-stroke engine, instead of a 4-stroke engine.

The 2-stroke engine is not nearly as efficient as a 4-stroke engine. It burns around twice as much gasoline per horsepower. But it delivers about half again as much horsepower for the same size and speed engine. For such machines as outboard motors and lawn mowers, the extra fuel used is not as important as the size and weight.

Just as the name says, the 2-stroke engine gets a power stroke for every two strokes of the piston, instead of one out of four.

To do this the fuel-air mixture must be pushed into the cylinder. The piston can't suck it in, because every time the piston moves down it gives a power stroke.

The 2-stroke engine has a small, tight case around the crank that acts as another cylinder. When the piston moves down, it compresses whatever is in this crankcase. When the piston moves up, it makes a suction in the crankcase.

The crankcase has a valve that lets the fuel-air mixture from the carburetor in, but won't let it out. When the piston moves up, fuel and air is sucked into the crankcase. When the piston moves down, the valve slams shut. The mixture gets compressed.

When the piston gets low enough, it uncovers a hole in the side of the cylinder. This hole leads to the exhaust pipe. The burned gases from the last power stroke begin to escape. The piston also uncovers another hole in the other side of the cylinder. This hole leads to the crankcase. The compressed fuel-air rushes into the cylinder and helps chase out the last of the exhaust.

This is the main reason why the 2-stroke engine is so inefficient. Fuel is being blown into the cylinder at the same time that the exhaust is being let out. They are bound to mix a little. Some of the fresh fuel goes out with the exhaust.

But the 2-stroke engine is cheaper and simpler to make. The two holes in the side of the cylinder take the place of complicated inlet and exhaust valves that have to be opened and closed by the crankshaft in a 4-stroke engine. Since the fuel-air mixture goes through the crankcase, lubricating oil is mixed with the fuel and keeps the crankshaft well oiled. This is why oil is mixed with the gas for an outboard motor. Most 4-stroke engines use complicated oiling systems. And since the 2-stroke engine gives a power stroke twice as often as a 4-stroke engine, it gives much more power for the same size and weight.

34

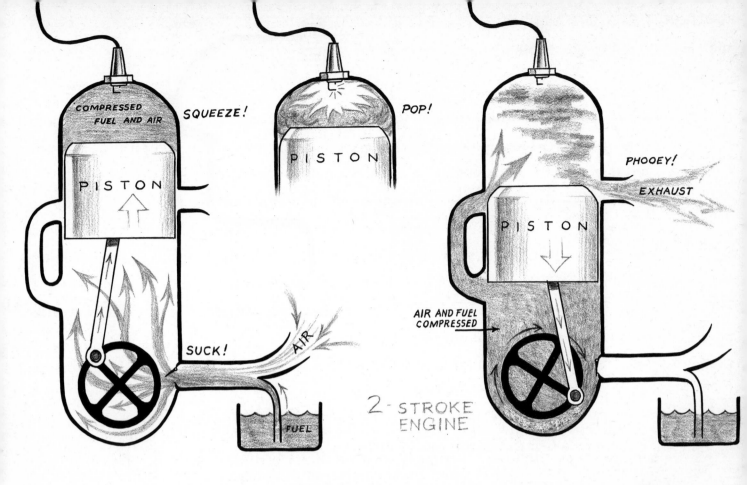

COMPRESSED FUEL AND AIR

SQUEEZE!

PISTON

POP!

PISTON

PHOOEY!

EXHAUST

PISTON

SUCK!

AIR

FUEL

2-STROKE ENGINE

AIR AND FUEL COMPRESSED

U. S. 1174090

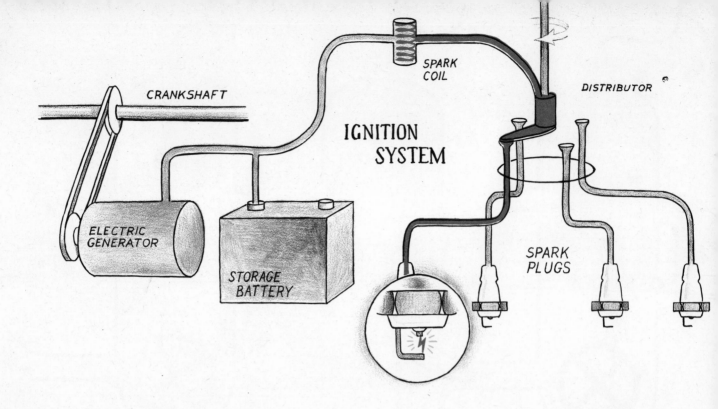

CRANKSHAFT

SPARK COIL

IGNITION SYSTEM

DISTRIBUTOR

ELECTRIC GENERATOR

STORAGE BATTERY

SPARK PLUGS

There are many other parts on modern gasoline engines. The ignition system is one of them. "Ignition" is simply a two-dollar word for "lighting." The electricity that makes a spark in the spark plugs, and lights the fuel, comes from a battery. A little spinning switch called a distributor sends electricity to each plug at the right time. The spark coil, a kind of transformer, steps up the battery voltage enough to make a spark. On most 2-stroke engines, a generator built right into the flywheel makes the electricity. Such a generator is called a magneto.

All engines have to be cooled. The many explosions inside the cylinders would get them red-hot if the heat were not carried away. Water in hollow jackets around the cylinders cools most engines. A pump keeps the water moving through the jackets and the radiator. The radiator is a network of tiny pipes that cools the water again after its trip through the cylinder jackets.

Airplane engines and many 2-stroke engines are cooled by fins on the cylinders. The fins make the surface of the metal much larger so more heat can leak away into the air.

Gasoline engines will not start by themselves as steam engines will. Fuel has to be put into the cylinder, compressed, and lit. Most engines are started by electric motors. Some of them are started by cranks or ropes wound around the flywheel.

Mr. Diesel's Engine

THERE is a clever and very important engine that really was invented by one man. His name was Rudolf Diesel, a German, and he patented his new engine in 1892.

Diesel knew that the secret of efficiency is the pressure at which the fuel is burned. The higher the compression, the more efficient the engine.

But you can't squeeze a gasoline-air mixture very much. When air is compressed, it gets hot. This would light the fuel before the piston reached the top of its stroke, and drive the crank backward. Even the best modern gasoline engines, using very high octane gasoline, can't compress the mixture more than to about one eighth of its volume. This is called a compression of 8:1.

Rudolf Diesel decided to turn the problem around. Suppose he used the heat of the compression to light the fuel, instead of a spark plug? But the fuel could not be mixed with the air while it was being compressed, or it would explode too soon. The fuel would have to be added at the last instant.

Diesel did just that. He built an engine that worked much like a gasoline engine, except that there was no carburetor and the compression in the cylinders was much greater. Just as the piston reached the top of the cylinder, a drop of fuel was injected, or forced in.

37

It worked. It worked so well that the Diesel engine is used today wherever great power and great fuel economy are needed. Diesel engines drive most large tractors, many trucks and busses. They power medium-sized ships and almost all submarines. They are chasing most steam locomotives from the rails.

*　　　*　　　*

The Diesel engine, for its size, is the most efficient practical engine we have.

Where a gasoline engine can compress up to about 8:1 if high-octane gas is used, a Diesel engine compresses at least 14:1 and often more. This high compression makes it about one-third efficient. A gasoline engine is about one-fourth efficient, and a steam engine only one-eighth.

The Diesel engine has other advantages. It uses heavier, cheaper oil than a gasoline engine. Diesel oil costs about half as much as gasoline, and an engine of the same horsepower will run about twice as long on a gallon. In some ways the Diesel engine is simpler, too. It has no carburetor, no ignition system.

But the Diesel engine costs a lot more than a gasoline engine. The parts have to be very strong and carefully made to stand the high compression. This also makes it much heavier than a gasoline engine.

In a Diesel engine plain air is sucked or blown into the cylinder, depending on whether it is a 2-stroke or 4-stroke Diesel. The air is compressed to about 550 pounds per square inch as the piston moves to the top. The compression makes the air red-hot, 1100 degrees.

When the piston reaches the top, a fuel injector sprays a drop of oil into the red-hot air. The injector is usually a tiny cylinder with a small piston. The oil is sprayed in through holes so tiny you cannot see them without a magnifying glass. The small holes break up the oil into a very fine spray.

When the oil hits the hot air, it begins burning. It burns more slowly than does the gasoline in a gas engine. This gives a smoother, slower explosion that gets more push and less bang out of the fuel.

The rest of the working is about the same as a gasoline engine. The burned gases are blown out the exhaust, fresh air is pumped in, and this is compressed again for the next power stroke. A 4-stroke engine does all this in the four strokes of the piston, while a 2-stroke engine needs a closed crankcase or other blower to supply the air and blow out the exhaust.

Most Diesel engines are cooled by water jackets. Since the Diesel is by nature a

38

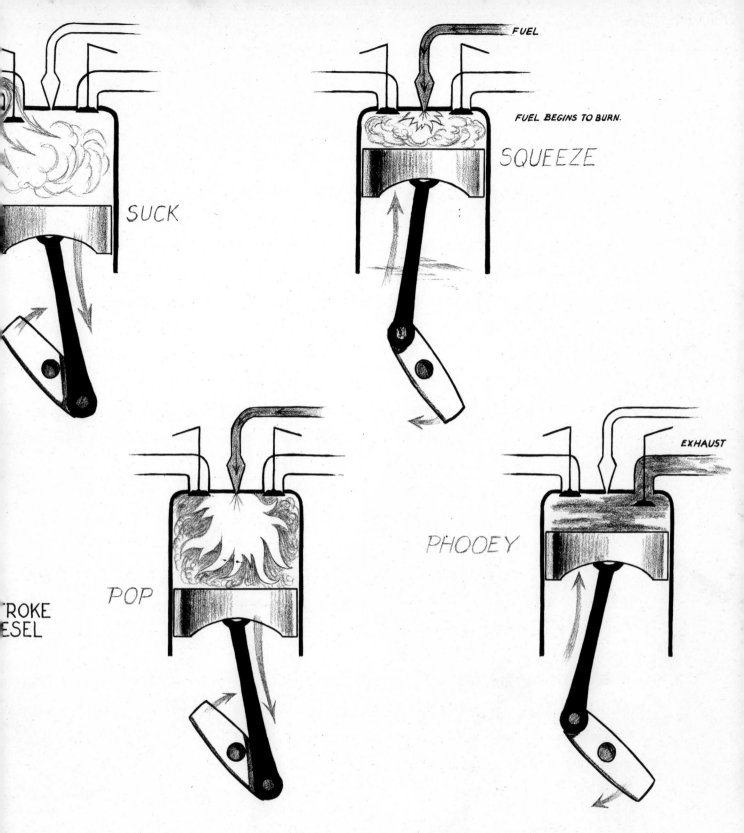

FUEL

FUEL BEGINS TO BURN.

SQUEEZE

SUCK

PHOOEY

EXHAUST

POP

STROKE
DIESEL

heavy, bulky engine, the extra weight of the water jacket doesn't hurt much. Diesel engines have to be started too, just like gasoline engines. They are harder to start because of the very high compression ratio. Some of them are started by small gasoline engines. Others are started by electric motors, or by compressed air from a tank which is pumped full again by the engine after it starts.

The Diesel engine seems to be about the final development of the piston-and-cylinder, or reciprocating (moving back and forth), engine.

Turbines, Old and New

THE reciprocating, or piston-and-cylinder, engine is good for lots of things. But it is definitely not good for high speeds. It vibrates and makes too much noise. And it wastes power, because the heavy pistons have to be stopped and started again at the end of every stroke.

Engineers searched for a long time for a good way of getting power from fuel in an engine that just went around and around instead of back and forth. The water wheel and the windmill did this, but the engineers were after better things.

The steam turbine was the natural answer, a sort of enclosed water wheel spun by steam pressure. Long ago a Greek named Hero had made a toy that spun by having steam spray out of little nozzles.

The problem was to make the turbine spin with enough power to do any work.

To get any sort of efficiency, a turbine should spin as fast as the steam that turns it. If there is too much difference between the speed of the steam and the speed of the turbine blades, the efficiency is very low.

Yet the steam can't be slowed down without lowering the pressure. Low-pressure steam doesn't do much work. If the turbine were speeded up enough to work well with high-pressure steam, it would fly to bits.

There seemed to be no answer.

An answer was found, though. Around 1885 an Englishman named Parsons worked out a way to use high-pressure steam and make it move slowly without losing power.

41

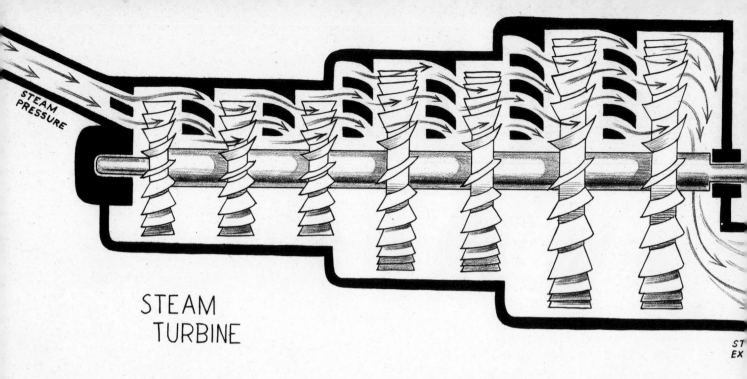

He did this by hooking up many turbine wheels right next to each other. Between each two turbine wheels there were nozzles that took the steam leaving one turbine and turned it back so that it pushed against the next one. All the turbine wheels were on the same shaft.

If there are 20 turbine wheels on the same shaft, with 20 nozzles between them, the steam loses only part of its pressure at each wheel. Since it drops just a little in pressure each time, it is not moving nearly as fast as if it dropped all its pressure at any one wheel.

Since the steam is moving more slowly, the turbine can be efficient at lower speeds. Actually the steam is still moving very fast, and turbines are very high-speed machines.

Such an arrangement is called a compound turbine.

Compound turbines are used in most large ships and in electric generating stations. A turbine is not quite as efficient as a Diesel or gasoline engine in small sizes, but it is very efficient in large sizes. And it can run on any sort of cheap fuel—coal or heavy oil or even wood, anything that will burn under the boiler.

*   *   *

There is a new kind of turbine that may soon take the place of many gasoline and Diesel engines. It is not very efficient now, but someday it will probably be as good as the Diesel engine. This is the gas turbine.

The gas turbine runs on the expansion of burned fuel and heated air, just as a steam turbine runs on the expansion of water into steam.

42

When fuel burns, the gases from the burning and the heated air expand. They drive the piston in a gasoline or Diesel engine. In a gas turbine, they rush out through a turbine wheel and make it spin.

The turbine needs a lot of air to be expanded by the heat and drive the turbine. This air is supplied by a many-bladed fan called a compressor. The compressor sucks in large quantities of air and pushes it into the chamber where the fuel is sprayed in and burned.

The compressor fan is turned by the turbine wheel, which also turns a shaft that does the work.

This is the sort of engine used by "turbo-prop" airplanes. The turbine wheel spins the propeller as well as the compressor.

Experiments have been made with gas turbines in automobiles and trucks. All the problems have not been solved, but the future looks bright. A turbine wheel the size of a salad plate will give a car as much horsepower as a V-8 engine. It will run on kerosene or diesel oil at half the cost of gasoline. It needs no complicated gears, which adjust the speed of a gasoline engine to the load.

The main problem is that the gases spinning the turbine are so hot that any ordinary metal such as steel is soon ruined. Special alloys, or mixtures of metals, are used. They are so expensive that the turbine wheel alone now costs more than the whole engine of an ordinary car.

But this problem will be solved. In 20 or 30 years the standard car may be equipped with a small, quiet, smooth-running gas turbine.

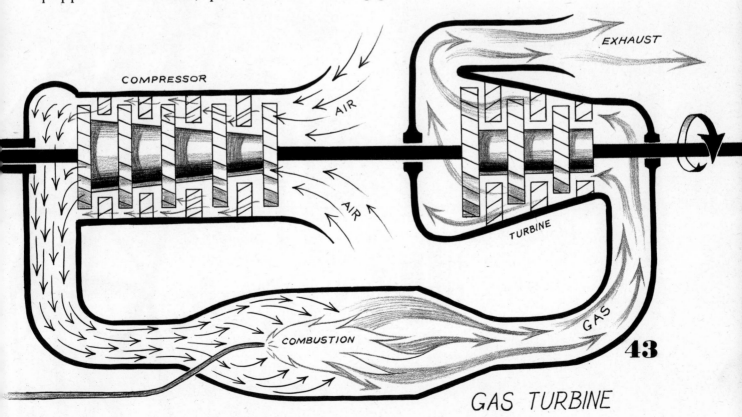

COMPRESSOR
AIR
AIR
EXHAUST
TURBINE
COMBUSTION
GAS

43

GAS TURBINE

Electricity: Carrying Power Around

BEFORE electricity was harnessed to carry power from one place to another, power had to be used right at its source.

Sawmills, flour mills, factories run by water wheels had to be located on the banks of rivers. Other factories had a steam engine chuffing away, with long drive shafts and belts to run the lathes or presses or looms.

Electricity has changed all this. A factory may be a hundred miles from its power source. It buys electricity to run its machines. And each machine has its own small, quiet motor, instead of flapping belts from overhead drive shafts.

Electricity is not a power source. The power comes from burning fuel, or water running downhill. This power is changed into electricity so that it can be carried around by wires.

*   *   *

You know just as much as scientists do about why electric motors and generators work. They know how, but they don't know why.

For some unknown reason an electric current flowing through a wire makes the wire act like a magnet. If the wire is coiled up, the magnetism of each turn of the coil adds to the magnetism of all the other turns, and the coil becomes a strong magnet.

Imagine such a coil with electricity flowing through it. Hold a real magnet near it. If the north pole of the real magnet is pointed at the south pole of the electric magnet, they will pull toward each other. If the two north poles or the two south poles are next to each other, the magnets will push each other away.

That is just how an electric motor works. Coils of wire are mounted on a shaft so they can turn. Magnets are placed near the ends of the coils. Electric current runs through the coils to make them push away from one magnet and pull toward another. As soon as they reach these magnets, the direction of the current is changed. The north and south poles of the coils change. Now the coils push away from the magnets they just reached and pull toward the ones they left.

The shaft, pulled and pushed around by the electric magnets, begins spinning. It has become an electric motor.

The motor changes the direction of the current by itself. Connections to the coils are mounted on the shaft. Wires rub against these connections. As the shaft turns, the wires keep touching different connections and change the direction of the current.

Most motors use coils of wire for both the spinning magnets and the fixed magnets too. Part of the electricity to run the motor is used to make the fixed magnets work. The motor is much stronger than it would be if only iron magnets were used.

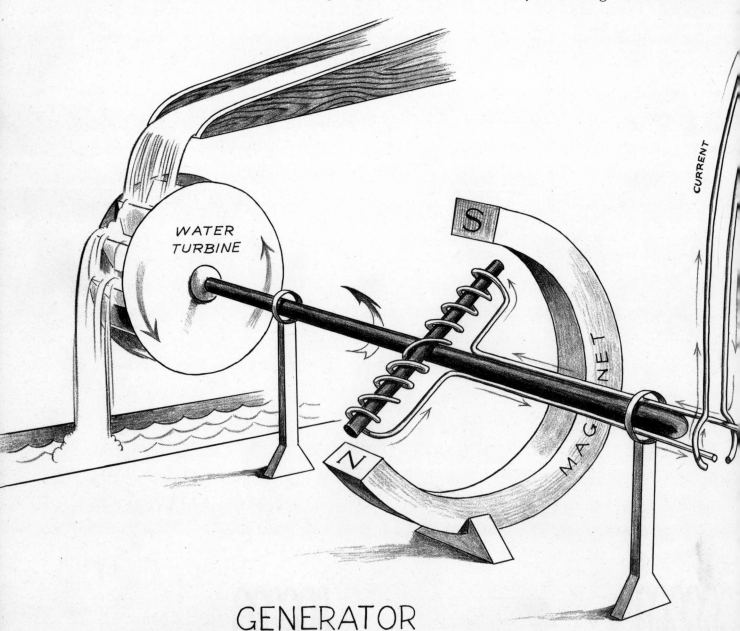

GENERATOR

MOTOR

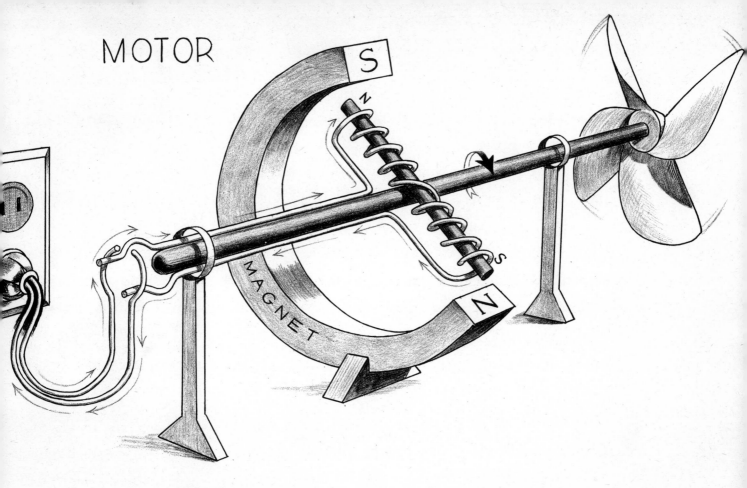

For the same unknown reason that an electric current makes a wire act like a magnet, moving a wire near a magnet makes electricity flow through the wire.

That is how generators work.

A generator is almost exactly like a motor. But instead of using electricity to spin the shaft and do work, the generator uses work to turn the shaft and make electricity.

The coils on the shaft, moving near the magnets, have electricity started in them. This electricity is drained off by the same sort of connections and rubbing wires used in motors. The electricity is sent through wires to whoever wants it and can pay for it.

The wonderful thing about electricity is that you can get power from fuel or running water in one place and use it in another. But we have also learned how to make the power in electricity do many other things besides turn motors. The power gives light in electric bulbs, heat in electric water heaters and electric stoves, and does other miraculous things in radios and television sets and telephones.

Without electricity you would need an engine in your basement to run your furnace blower, the washing machine, the clothes drier. You would need another engine in the kitchen to run the refrigerator pump, the mixer, and the ventilating fan. All these machines now have their own small, handy electric motors. When you plug them in, you are really plugging them directly into the large water turbines of the hydroelectric station or steam turbines of the steam-electric station.

Electricity also lets us control power better. Many navy ships are powered by steam turbines. But the turbines, to be efficient, must run much faster than the propellers. So instead of connecting the turbines to the propellers, the turbines often run generators. The generators are connected to motors that turn the propellers. The motors can be speeded up or slowed down without changing the speed of the turbines.

Submarines often use the same sort of electric motors, though their main power source is usually a Diesel engine. The atomic submarines *Nautilus* and *Sea Wolf* use steam turbines that drive generators. Most Diesel locomotives use electric motors to turn the wheels, with electricity from generators turned by the Diesel engines. Some new busses also use this system. The advantages are smoothness, quiet, and better control, even though it costs more.

Some railroads, of course, run on electricity alone. They get it through overhead trolleys or through the "third rail" that carries the current and gives it to the train through a connection that rubs along it. The power that drives these trains really comes from running water or burning fuel. The electricity merely carries the power to the train.

Jets and Rockets

IN THE last twenty years airplanes have begun to use a different kind of engine that does its work invisibly. It does not turn a propeller. It just pushes, sometimes with no moving parts at all.

This is the type of engine that will launch the satellite station and may some-day push a rocket ship to the moon.

Jet or rocket power depends on the fact that when you push something, the force of your push shoves you backward.

When you jump hard from a box, the box falls over backward. When you shoot a rifle, you get a kick. When you squirt water from a hose, the hose pushes back.

This is called reaction.

An airplane propeller, or a ship propeller, uses reaction too. The propeller is a fan pushing air or water in one direction. The propeller gets pushed in the other direction by reaction.

Jets and rockets are called reaction motors. They push gas in one direction. For every pound of push they give the gas, they get pushed half a pound in the other direction. Gas isn't very heavy, but reaction motors push a lot of it, and they push it hard.

* * *

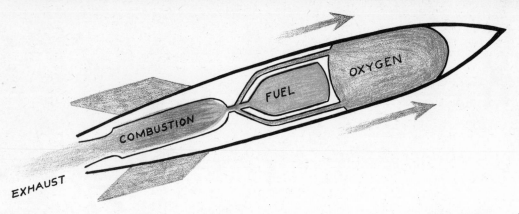

ROCKET

A rocket squirts gas from burning fuel and oxygen. It is the only kind of motor that will work in outer space where there is no air, because the push does not come from gas pressing against air. The push comes from the reaction to the shove the rocket gives the gas. Rockets drive guided missiles, the proposed satellite, any space ships we may build, and Fourth-of-July skyrockets.

A jet motor works the same way as the rocket, except that it does not carry its own oxygen. It gets its oxygen from the air. It won't work in space where there is no air, but for airplanes it's better because there's no oxygen to carry around.

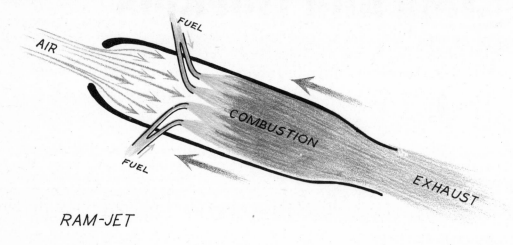

RAM-JET

The simplest jet is the ram-jet. It has no moving parts at all. It won't work until it is moving fast enough to "ram" air in through the opening in front and build compression inside. Fuel is sprayed in and burned. The gases and heated air expand and rush out the nozzle in back.

Since it pushes gas out the back, the ram-jet gets pushed forward.

The ram-jet will not start until it's moving fast enough to "ram." It has no fans or cylinders to build compression. So up to now it has been more or less a toy. For extra speed in combat, or planes to be launched from other planes, or planes to be started by rockets, it may someday be important.

The jet planes you see today, and are likely to see in the near future, are turbo-jets.

The turbo-jet gets its name from "turbine." It is just like the gas turbine, except that only part of the power of the hot gases is used to spin the compressor fan. Most of the power of the gases is allowed to escape in order to push the jet forward by reaction. In fact, the turbo-jet was developed from the gas turbine.

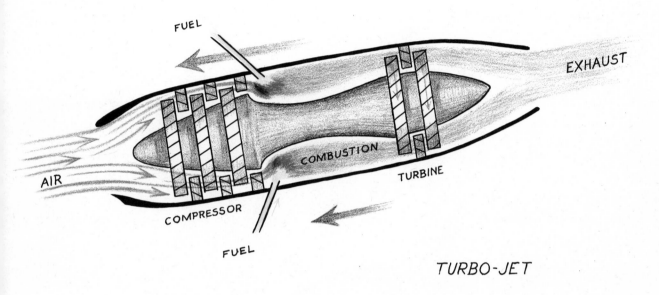

TURBO-JET

One other type of jet is the pulse-jet. This has a one-way valve in front that lets air in but not out. The valve lets air in until there is enough compression for good burning. Fuel is sprayed in and a spark plug lights it. The explosion slams the valve shut and shoves the jet forward. The valve opens again to let in more air.

The pulse-jet is simpler than the turbo-jet and works at lower speeds than the ram-jet, but it isn't very efficient. It drove the "buzz-bombs" of World War II and is used on some model airplanes, but that is about all. It makes a lot of noise, too, because of the explosions.

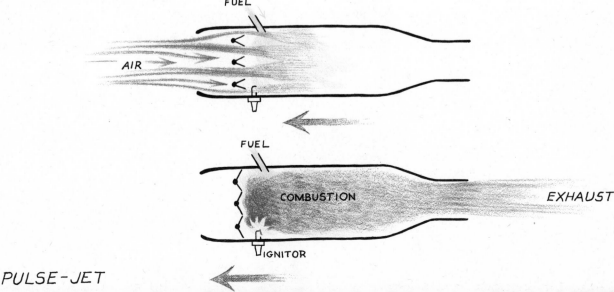

PULSE-JET

Besides pushing planes, jets have been used to push speedboats, racing cars, and helicopter blades.

Jets are efficient only at high speeds. To get any sort of efficiency, the jet should move forward half as fast as it shoots out the gases. The gases are shoved out at very high speeds, so jets waste a lot of fuel at ordinary speeds. But they burn kerosene and other cheap fuels, so except for flying range their inefficiency does not hurt too much.

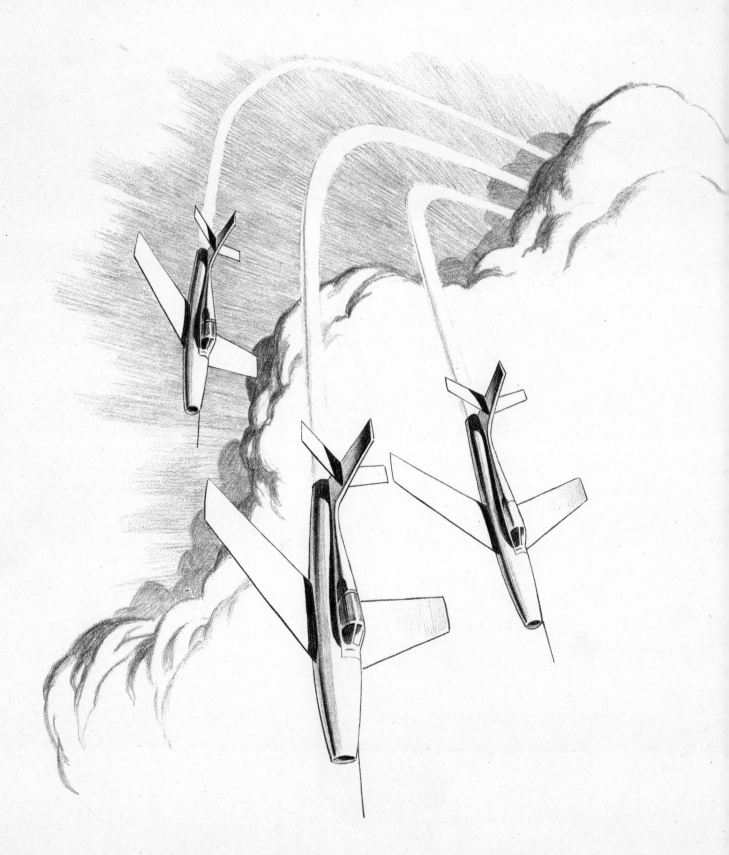

Power from the Sun

ALL ways of getting power—running water, wind, and burning fuels—depend on the sun.

Most of the engines and motors depend on coal or oil. These are called "fossil fuels," since they are made of living things that died millions of years ago and have

53

become fossils. We are using up those fuels. The day will come when all our coal and oil will be burned up.

Since the power stored in these fuels came from the sun, scientists have often wondered about ways to use the power in the sunlight falling on the earth today.

There are many ways to do this. "Solar houses," homes with big windows planned so that sunlight will help heat them in the winter, are using power from the sun for heat. In warm climates water is sometimes run through pipes on the roof so it will be hot for washing and bathing. Experiments have been made with heating water or chemicals in this way, and storing them to heat houses in the winter.

54

But heating homes is only a small part of the power we need. We need power to turn shafts and drive things, from automobiles and ships to airplanes and factory machines.

Since sunlight is hot, and can be focused or directed by mirrors to make one spot very very hot, many people have tried to run steam engines with steam made by the heat of sunlight. Some of them have succeeded, but the power has always been small compared to the cost of building and taking care of the equipment.

Usually a sun steam plant has a big curved mirror to focus the sunlight on a small boiler. Water in this boiler is turned to steam by the heat, and is piped to a regular steam engine or turbine. When the sun goes behind a cloud or night falls, of course, the boiler stops working and so does the engine.

The most promising way of getting power right from the sun was invented a few years ago by Bell Telephone Laboratories. The new "solar battery" makes electricity from sunlight, with no moving parts of any kind.

The solar battery is a piece the size of a quarter of very pure silicon, the substance from which sand is made. It has been treated in such a way that it has an electric barrier, or gate. Electricity can flow through this barrier in one direction, but not the other. Sunlight hitting the silicon starts electricity moving around in it. Some of the electricity drifts through the barrier and can't get back. This makes too much electricity on one side of the barrier and not enough on the other. If the two sides are connected by a wire, current will flow through it to even up the electricity. This current gives a little power. Many of these batteries together give more power.

So far, the solar battery has made only enough electricity to work a telephone. It is being tried out in sunny parts of the country to run farm telephones. It makes enough extra electricity when the sun is shining to charge a storage battery, which runs the telephones at night.

56

The two problems about the solar battery are the small amount of power it gives, and the cost of making it. The silicon must be purified until there is less than one part of impurity to a billion parts of silicon. This is very expensive, far more expensive than making an ordinary battery.

But all problems can be solved. Someday the solar battery may generate much of our electricity.

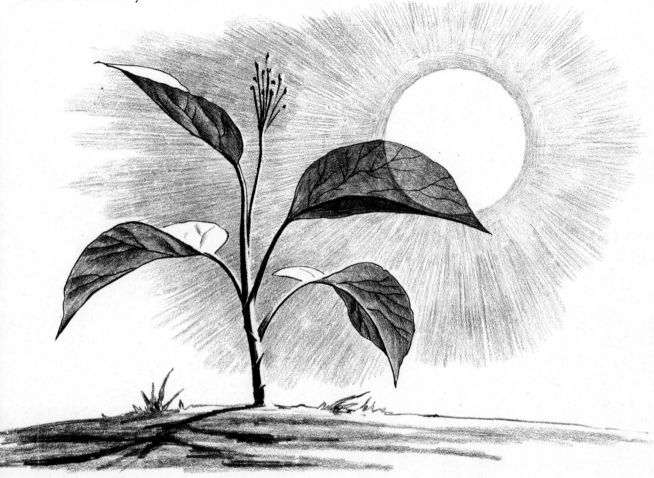

Many scientists think that the most practical way to get power from the sun is to use nature's own way more efficiently. The magic process of photosynthesis, by which living plants lock power from the sun into sugar, has never been equaled by man. If quicker and better ways of changing this sugar into fuel can be invented, and quick-growing crops developed, we may be able to solve a lot of our fuel problems. During the Second World War, the Germans learned to run engines with alcohol made from sugar beets. Many cities supply homes with artificial gas made from garbage and sewage. Fuel alcohol has been made from wood, too.

Someday, perhaps, fields of special fuel crops will replace the "fossil fuels" we will have used up.

Atomic Power

ALL power comes from the sun.

But we are even learning how to make small suns of our own, and get power from them!

We call this atomic energy.

The power we get from the sun, which runs our motors and engines and even our muscles, is atomic power. The sun shines because it is changing atoms into other atoms. The change releases fantastic amounts of power, millions of times as much power as burning.

We have already learned to make atomic power in a crude and roundabout way.

First came the atomic bomb. The people who invented it knew that the incredible power they had released could be harnessed to give peaceful power. Today that power is driving the submarines *Nautilus* and *Sea Wolf*, and is about to generate electricity in several parts of our country.

Then came the hydrogen bomb, even more powerful than the atomic bomb. We have reason to believe that the time will come when men have tamed the fury of the hydrogen bomb and made it turn their motors.

The atomic bomb and the hydrogen bomb both use atomic energy, but they work in opposite ways.

The power for both comes from the atom. Every substance is made of atoms. Imagine a tiny sun with planets revolving around it. The sun is the nucleus. It is a tightly packed mass of protons and neutrons, tiny particles about which we do not know very much. The little planets whirling around the nucleus are electrons. They are smaller than protons and neutrons, but that is about all we know about them.

The whole atom—protons, neutrons, electrons, and all—is so tiny that it takes about a hundred *billion* of them to make the point of a pin. Nobody has ever seen an atom. It is much too small. But we know how they are built because of the way they act.

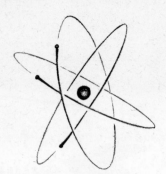

Every substance is made of the same kind of protons, neutrons, and electrons. The number of each makes the atom the kind of substance it is.

Hydrogen is the lightest element of all. It has only one proton in its nucleus, and only one electron whirling around it.

Uranium is the heaviest natural element of all. It has 92 protons in its nucleus, a number of neutrons, and 92 electrons as planets.

But there is no difference in the protons, neutrons, and electrons of different atoms.

*   *   *

The atomic bomb is made of a special kind of uranium whose atoms can be changed into other atoms. The protons, neutrons, and electrons are torn apart and put together again to make new atoms such as krypton and barium. When all the new atoms are weighed, about one thousandth of the original weight of the uranium is gone. Part of the matter has been turned into energy as heat and light.

The uranium atoms are made to change by adding an extra neutron to the nucleus of one of the atoms. This extra neutron is more than the atom can stand. It breaks apart. Some of the neutrons from its nucleus hit other atoms and they break apart too, releasing more neutrons which hit still other atoms. This is known as the chain reaction.

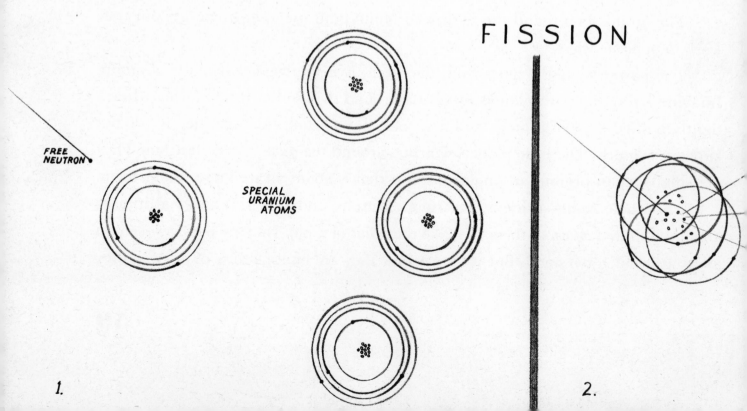

FISSION

FREE NEUTRON

SPECIAL URANIUM ATOMS

1.

2.

The atomic bomb does all this in a flash. The explosion is almost unbelievably powerful. But scientists have learned to make the same thing happen slowly in an atomic pile. The pile gets hot as uranium atoms break up into other atoms and part of the substance is turned into energy.

The heat of the atomic pile is used to turn water into steam. The steam spins a turbine, which turns a generator to make electricity. This is a crude and roundabout way of getting atomic energy, but it works. And an atomic pile, acting as the "fire" for the boiler, may keep working for years on a small amount of atomic "fuel."

Atomic power can be very dangerous. The pile sends out deadly, mysterious "radioactive" rays. It must be shielded with thick walls of lead or concrete to keep the people working with it safe. These rays also make other substances "radioactive." These are valuable in treating certain illnesses and in research.

One radioactive substance may give us a way to turn atomic energy directly into electricity, without boilers and turbines and generators. RCA has invented an atomic battery that works much like the solar battery. The rays sent out by a radioactive substance make electricity flow in a piece of silicon just as sunlight does. The same sort of barrier lets the electricity flow in one direction, but not in the other. The extra electricity on one side of the barrier will flow through a wire to the other side, where there is a lack of electricity.

So far the atomic battery is too weak to be practical. The solar battery is thousands of times more powerful.

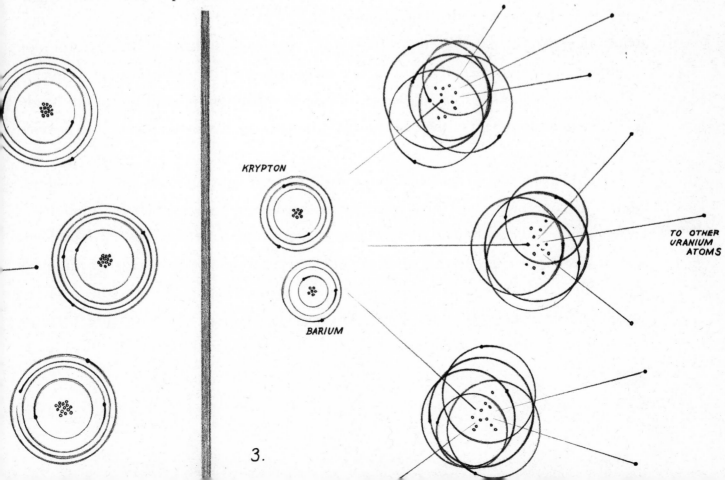

KRYPTON

BARIUM

TO OTHER URANIUM ATOMS

3.

FUSION

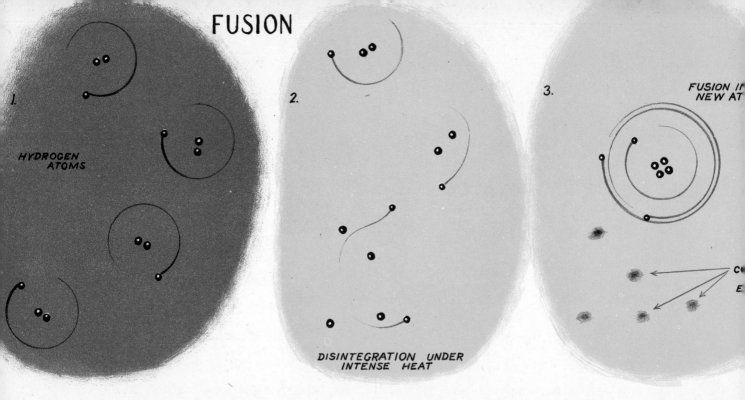

1. HYDROGEN ATOMS

2. DISINTEGRATION UNDER INTENSE HEAT

3. FUSION INTO NEW ATOMS

The way in which uranium gives atomic power is called "fission." This means that big, heavy atoms are broken up into smaller atoms. The hydrogen bomb uses the opposite process of "fusion." In fusion several atoms of a simple, light substance are broken up and their parts are combined to make one heavier atom. Just as in fission, part of the substance disappears and turns into heat and light.

Fusion gives the sun its power. The sun is a gigantic hydrogen bomb. The hydrogen atoms are constantly being torn apart and their protons and electrons combined into heavier atoms. The sun is so big that the hydrogen will last for millions of years more.

The light atoms are made to break up and combine into heavier, more complicated atoms by simply getting them hot enough. The sun has a temperature of somewhere between 50,000,000 and 180,000,000 degrees. The heat of a blowtorch, for comparison, is around 2000 degrees. The sun is around fifty *thousand* times as hot!

The hydrogen bomb is made to explode by setting off a uranium bomb inside it. The tremendous heat of the uranium bomb starts the hydrogen fusing into heavier atoms of helium.

The heat needed to start fusion is more than any substance we know can stand. Metals not only melt, they turn to vapor at these temperatures. So even though we know how to make such heat, the problem of controlling it for power is not yet solved.

It has been suggested that a stream of electrons from an atom-smasher might be able to heat a tiny bit of hydrogen hot enough to start fusing. If the hydrogen were in the middle of an empty tank filled with another gas that would not fuse, perhaps the walls of the tank could be kept cool enough so they would not melt.

Another way to prevent fusing hydrogen from melting its tank might be to send a very strong electric current through it. Scientists think that the magnetism of a strong enough current could pull the hydrogen into a very thin thread, away from the sides of the tank.

The Atomic Energy Commission is working on this project now. Early guesses are that the problem may be solved by around 1975, though it may be sooner or later.

*   *   *

If hydrogen power is developed, it will be the most important invention in the story of power since a bright cave man first decided to let running water carry his logs for him.

We may use up every other form of fuel. Even uranium is hard to find and expensive. But we can get all the hydrogen we would ever need from ordinary water.

Hydrogen power will open up a fabulous new world to us. Many countries are backward because they have no water or too much water, and no coal or oil. Hydrogen power can water deserts and level mountains, drain lakes and build islands. Many scarce minerals we need for our complicated technical world are found in plenty in sea water, but they can be separated only with large amounts of power. Magnesium is one metal that right now is taken from sea water in some places where power is cheap enough. Hydrogen power can mine the oceans. It can move goods from one place to another more cheaply and faster, and run the machines to produce homes and cars and clothes and other needs for lower prices.

Who knows—fusing hydrogen may push the first space ship to the moon!

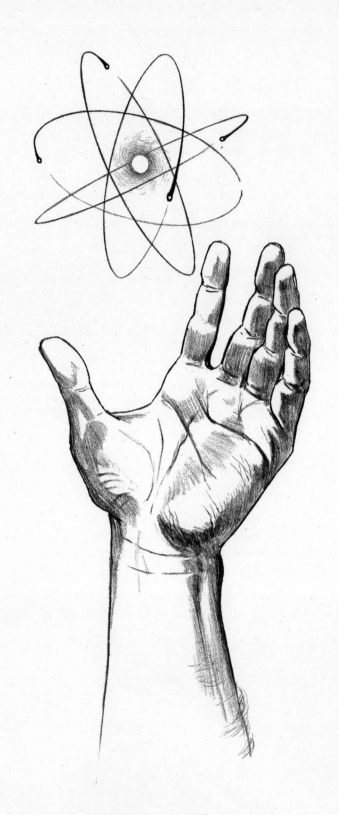

1938 F.W.